Spirituality/Christian/Self-Help/Biographies

I0098315

BRIGHT LIGHT THERAPY

b
COLLEGE BOY
PUBLISHING
"We Breed Bestsellers"

ISBN: 978-1-944110-33-8

Published in Dallas, TX, by College Boy Publishing. College Boy Publishing is a division of The College Boy Company & ArmaniValentino.com. To order wholesale or bulk orders of this book, please contact the publisher directly at collegeboypublishing@gmail.com or call 972-781-8404.

Autographed copies of this book may be ordered directly from www.SherrondaBowman.com.

Please allow up to 7-14 Business Days for delivery.

Sherronda Bowman is available for keynote addresses, workshops, panel discussions, consultations, and radio & television interviews by emailing sherrondabowman@gmail.com or by calling 706-604-9569.

Printed in the United States of America

08 09 10 11 12 SBAV 5 4 3 2 1

Bright Light Therapy
Stories on Spiritual Living
Told from the Heart

by
Sherronda Bowman

Edited by **Latangela Vann** & **Armani Valentino**
for College Boy Publishing

Published for Print and Digital formats by **Armani Valentino**
for College Boy Publishing

Cover Design by **Armani Valentino**
for College Boy Publishing

TABLE OF CONTENTS

Introduction

INTRODUCTION

Light is made from atoms that get excited. When an atom absorbs energy, the electrons extend upward to a higher position. The electrons become so excited that they have to move back to their neutral location where they stabilize, and in return, give back the energy that was absorbed. The flashes of light we see are the result of photons, a collection of the energy given back from the electrons (www.brooklyncuny.edu/bc/ahp/LAD). In relation to the spiritual realm, I would like to invite you to get just as excited about our personal light, as the atoms get when producing physical light. As Christians, we should be able to absorb the light of life given to us by Jesus Christ and be able to share that precious gift with others. In this novel, I would like to make the connection between physical and spiritual light.

"And the earth was without form, and void; and darkness was upon the face of the deep. And the Spirit of God moved upon the face of the waters. And God said, Let there be light: and there was light" (King James Version Bible, Gen. 1. 2-3). Each one of us are 'void' and 'dark' without the spirit of the Lord. I would also like to discuss light and remind everyone how it reappears and reminds us that every day is new. We are given a second chance to seek the light: "That they should seek the Lord, if haply they might feel after him, and find him, though he be not far from every one of us..." (Acts 17:27); walk in the light: "For the Lord God *is a sun and shield: the Lord will give grace and glory: no good thing will he withhold from them that walk uprightly*" (Psa. 84:11); *and to eventually- become a light: "The night is far spent, the day is at hand: let us therefore cast off the works of darkness, and let us put on the armour of light*" (Rom. 13:12).

Today, in the medical field, light therapy is a way to treat seasonal affective disorders and other conditions by exposure to artificial light. Light therapy is a treatment that may help with depression, jet lag, sleep disorders, and helps reset your biological clock, which is responsible for sleeping and waking, according to WebMD. It is my intention to use 2 Peter 1: 5-15 as a guide to viewing light because, "…in light therapy, optometric phototherapy is a safe application of selected visible light frequencies through the eyes" according to brainworldmagazine.com (https://www.brainworldmagazine.com/syntonics-colored-light-therapy-for-balance/).

We are able to see colors through light. The Merriam-Webster dictionary defines color as "a phenomenon of light or visual perception that enables one to differentiate otherwise identical objects" (https://www.merriam-webster.com/dictionary/color). When light shines on an object, some colors bounce off of the object and others are absorbed by it. Our eyes can only see the colors that bounce off or are reflected off of an object. As Christians, we only see our true colors when we go through various trials and tribulations, the gray areas of our lives. I encourage you to move beyond black and white and let your light shine in vivid hues. Your true colors are exposed whether you want them to be or not. Sometimes, we are unaware of what colors we possess until we are introduced to these gray areas. Our eyes are the windows of the soul. "But if thine eye be evil, thy whole body shall be full of darkness. If therefore the light that is in thee be darkness, how great is that darkness!" (Matt. 6:23).

Chapter 1

Faith

Red

Red is a very intense color. It symbolizes blood & fire, strength & power, determination & sacrifice, passion & desire, and love & war. In my opinion, Faith is represented by the color red. "...Faith is the substance of things hoped for, the evidence of things not seen..." (Hebrews 11:1); it is the seed from which all other beams of light will grow. Not only can light help your physical and emotional well-being, it will also help your soul; granting you with strength of mind.

Jesus Christ is the ultimate light, he is not only the son of our heavenly father, but he is the daystar of our souls. He shed his blood for you and I- that's love. He had so much passion in his purpose that he went to Hades and defeated death (Eph. 4:8-10, 1 Cor. 15:55). Keep in mind that Christ did not go to Hell. Hades is the holding place for those who have rejected the light and have lived a life of darkness, and Hell is the *final resting place for them after the Judgment takes place. It is important to me that you know and understand that once you go to Hades, there is no turning back.*

Walking in the light is not always going to be rewarded on this side of life. The way our world works today, sometimes you are punished for doing the right thing. Though you might feel intimidated because of the wickedness of the world, stay focused, stand firm, and know that you are special. Have faith in God and believe that "...great is he that is in you, than he that is in the world" (1 John 4:4), because our life does not belong to us. Everything we have, and are, and will ever become is for the glory and honor of God.

Satan only wants to use our past against us. Do not give into evil desires. We can't change yesterday, and tomorrow is not promised. Focus on the things that are happening now because you may not have another chance.

I once heard a sermon titled "Kissing Calves" referring to Exodus 32. It was about Moses and his journey to write the Ten Commandments. When the Israelites grew tired of waiting for him, they created golden calf idols and worshipped them. The minister explained that you should not have anything before God; not children, money, cars or clothes, etc. I was so afraid. At the time, I was a young mother, and I came to the realization that I might love my son more than I love God. I felt that I couldn't seek the light, walk in the light, or be a light to others if I put my child before God.

While at the grocery store one day, I overheard a woman talking about how she never had children and had always wanted them. I immediately thought of the sermon preached to me and felt convicted to test my own faith. With my six-month old son in tow, I followed her to her home and observed how she lived. After ten minutes passed, I looked at my sleeping son (he was so content), put him in a bassinet, placed him on her doorstep, rang the doorbell, and ran away. When she opened the door, the woman saw me running and yelled out to me, "Sweetheart! Is this your baby?"

Chapter One—Red

Crying and sobbing, I ran back towards the woman's bellowing echoes and said, "Yes ma'am." My heart has never been filled with so much joy. I knew in my heart that I was going to have my baby, but I felt I needed to initiate the process of building my faith, trusting in God, and understanding that God will never take second place to anyone or anything. If God is second place in your life, then he is not in your life.

Years later, when my son was in kindergarten, I was in desperate need of a job. At the time, my only means of transportation was a rental car which I couldn't use for long. I drove to my husband's job where the rental company was scheduled to pick up the car. When I got there, my husband asked if I could pick our son up from school because he was ill. When I arrived at the school, I went to my son but something was wrong-he could not walk and he was running a high temperature of 104 degrees. I immediately took my son to the hospital. After being there for a while, the doctors pulled me aside and informed me that my son had been diagnosed with spinal meningitis. There are two kinds of spinal meningitis; one is viral and could easily be treated, and the other is a chronic disease.

My head was spinning. When my husband arrived at the hospital, our church minister was with him. They spent several hours praying over my child. Overwhelmed, I went home to get clothes and other provisions so that I could spend the night with my son. In the process of doing this, my neighbor sensed that something was wrong, and asked what was troubling me. When I explained to her what had happened, she began to sob. I looked at her confused, unsure why she was sobbing. Through her tears, she told me that she also had a child with the same condition, and he was in a nursing home. She looked me in the eyes and told me, "I'm sorry to tell you, but your child will never be able to walk again."

I looked back into her eyes and told her firmly, "No. I don't mean any harm, but my son *will be able to walk." With that being said, she quietly walked back to her apartment, and I rushed back to the hospital.*

After I was settled in, the doctor knocked on the door and entered the room. He sat next to me and explained that he would have to do another spinal tap on my son in order to determine the type of meningitis. I stood up, went into the bathroom, and closed the door. The next few moments in the corner of the bathroom, would be between me and the Lord. I placed myself at the altar (the bathroom corner) and prayed; I asked God for my child to be delivered and for the diagnoses to be the kind that could be cured. There came a point in my prayer when I had to ask the Lord to interpret my thoughts and feelings to God. I was in such tremendous pain for my child, that I could not form the words to complete my prayer. After about an hour in prayer, when I had complete peace, I stood up from my altar, washed my face and laid down. "Likewise the Spirit also helpeth our infirmities: for we know not what we should pray for as we ought: but the Spirit itself maketh intercession for us with groanings which cannot be uttered. And he that searcheth the hearts knoweth what *is the mind of the Spirit, because he maketh intercession for the saints according to the will of God." (Rom. 8:26).*

Once I was comfortable, there was another knock on the door. The doctor came back in and informed me of the test results. The Lord delivered my son. The doctor confirmed he had viral meningitis, which could be treated, and we would be going home in a few days. I thanked the doctor, and when he was gone I began praising and thanking God for showing his mercy and grace to my son.

When we were ready to go home, I recollected on how kind, patient and understanding the hospital staff was to me during my stay. Before we left the hospital, I asked for an employment application (I was still looking for a job). Though I was blessed to have my son safe and in good health, the Lord saw fit that my blessings should be extended. A few weeks later, I received a call from the hospital, and was blessed with a job as a triage nurse. I was now granted the responsibility of greeting other parents with sick children and comforting them in their time of worry and fear. It is true- "For as the heavens are higher than the earth, so are my ways higher than your ways, and my thoughts higher than your thoughts" (Isaiah 55:9).

Now this particular story is shorter than the others, but it has the same meaning. It was the year 2004 and I learned that my beloved stepfather passed away. At the time, we lived in two different states. Without question, I wanted to travel in order to pay my last respects. However, as fate would have it, an awful storm was headed straight for my destination. The media and emergency departments were encouraging the locals to evacuate the city. In my heart, I was determined and decided to step out on faith and continue with my travel plans.

I called my husband and told him the car was being prepared for my journey. He reiterated about the storm that was to come and I assured him that the Lord would see me through. After all, my stepfather had provided for and loved me as his own since I was a child. As I prayed to the Lord, I could hear the news in the background talking about the bad weather. I began walking around the building, praying to myself and getting strange looks along the way. Once the car was finished, the mechanic came to me, ready to receive his pay. As I walked inside, the TV was still on and I heard the reporter say that the storm was no longer headed to my destination, but to another location far away. It was then that I realized God had placed a rainbow in my life.

"…for verily I say unto you, If ye have faith as a grain of mustard seed, ye shall say unto this mountain, Remove hence to yonder place; and it shall remove; and nothing shall be impossible unto you" (King James Version, Matt. 17:20). If we would just show the faith of a mustard seed, we can say unto the mountain, 'Move!'

Chapter One—Red

The bright red light of faith is a spiritual treatment for ailments that only God can heal. Only this element of light can penetrate through intangible things. When the weather is rough, the red light of faith shines brightly through. Remember, your faith *has to be present, even when there is no evidence that things are going to work out. Faith had entered my life (red), and it would never be the same.*

Chapter 2

Virtue

Purple

The color purple symbolizes nobility, humility, wealth, and moral uprightness. It is an emblem of royalty or high rank. "But ye *are a chosen generation, a royal priesthood, an holy nation, a peculiar people; that ye should shew forth the praises of him who hath called you out of darkness into his marvelous light" (1 Peter 2:9).*

Once, someone asked why the moral fabric of the world is so dark. I told them because virtue has become so old fashioned. As defined in the Merriam-Webster Dictionary, virtue is "...a particular moral excellence..." (https://www.merriam-webster.com/dictionary/virtue). The world we live in today is not as virtuous as it should be. Some people today use manipulation and dishonesty for financial gain. In my community, some women get married with the intent of divorce and alimony in mind; both women and men use the government to get money for disability purposes when they are not actually disabled. These examples are of a dishonest mind and spirit and are not right in the sight of the Lord. We should only use resources like these if they are absolutely necessary, not for financial gain.

On the other hand, as negative situations present themselves, we ought to look at them with strength and courage; the spirit of God is still moving in your life so don't be deceived or trust your void feelings. "Have ye not known? Have ye not heard? Hath it not been told to you from the beginning? have ye not understood from the foundations of the earth? It is he that sitteth upon the circle of the earth..." (Isaiah 40:21).

I remember the story of a king who ruled over a small village. He was told that someone had been stealing from the town square. The king made an announcement, telling the people that if or when the thief was caught, the punishment would be a public beating. Shortly after this announcement the thief was caught, but it was the king's mother. The king was in shock, but nothing could be done because the consequence had already been set. He loved his mother unconditionally, however he just watched as the people took his beloved mother to the middle of the town square. Just as the guard raised the whip over his head, the king shouted, "Stop!" He walked towards his mother, ripped off his shirt and took her place for the beating. Living a virtuous life will always cost you something; because of virtue, we are able to "...sit together in heavenly places in Christ Jesus" (Ephesians 2:6).

When I lived in Florida, I was newly engaged and my wedding date had to be changed because my fiancè was to be inducted in the wrestling hall of fame at John Carroll University. We were married two weeks later. My husband worked in the automotive industry at the time, and was feeling discouraged about his job because his overseers wanted him to lie about certain products and sales information. As a newly baptized Christian, my husband felt it was not right and expressed his concerns to his supervisors. Because he was well-liked, they suggested he take a week off to search for a new job instead of firing him. While on a job interview, the owner observed him through a double sided mirror, watching the way he helped customers. A week later, the owner decided to give my husband the job and asked him to relocate to Atlanta, Georgia, where he would manage a busier shop.

At the same time, I was working at the blood bank. Like my husband, I was a new Christian, and the congregation I was a part of was protesting the blood bank where I worked. They were protesting because before drawing blood, they would ask people if they had been to Africa or Haiti recently, and the congregation thought it was prejudiced. I had no idea this situation was going on until a member from my congregation came in one day to give blood. My supervisors found out I was a member of the same congregation and terminated me from my job.

Once we moved to Atlanta, my husband settled into his job, and our family joined a new church. The congregation was predominately white. You would think that we wouldn't have any problems with race in the Lord's church, but there was a member of the congregation, an elder, who was prejudice towards my husband. He spoke to the church leader, and told them that he and his family did not want a black man praying over them. He threatened to leave the church if they continued to let my husband take part in worship services. Because of the congregation's virtue, they stood up to the member, gave him an address book and told him to find another church home. After this incident, the church continued to show love to our family.

Bright Light Therapy

By this time, I was pregnant, nesting like a mother bird, and buying new things for both the baby and our home. While I was busy making everything baby proof, I told my husband I had the feeling that something new was about to happen in our lives. I mentioned this feeling to him quite a few times, but he just kept telling me, "Of course! You are pregnant and about to have our baby."

I told him, "Yes, I know, but I can just feel it...something else is about to happen." Well, something did happen. My daughter was born; I was so happy and overjoyed to have my little girl. Her birth took my attention away from all of the negativity surrounding our family. My joy soon shifted into worry when my husband's place of employment caught fire. Once again he was out of a job. The Lord, like always, was looking out for us because two days later my husband had found a new job as a photographer.

"Ask, and it shall be given unto you: seek, and ye shall find; knock, and it shall be opened unto you" (Matthew 7:7). There was a knock on the door. There was a strange man standing at the door asking for my husband. He told me that there was another job opportunity available for him in Columbus. We thought he was referring to Columbus, Ohio, because we had never heard of Columbus, Georgia. A few weeks later we decided to relocate, and the owner of the new shop agreed to rent us a spacious, three bedroom home made of brick. The landscaping was beautiful, and the neighborhood was friendly.

One stormy day as I was carrying my groceries to my apartment, I saw a young man sitting on the stairs crying. I asked him what was wrong, and he began to sob harder. I invited this stranger into my home and began to talk with him. I learned that his name was Michael, and he had just been diagnosed with cancer. Concerned for his soul, I asked him if he would like to have bible study with us, and he said yes. He came to bible studies that were held with a few members of our congregation at our home. About a month later he was baptized. I explained to him that now, his name was written in the Lamb's Book of Life- you know, the book that God is going to look at during the judgment.

My family had grown close to Michael. One day his mother came to visit from New York; she seemed to be a dedicated, loving mother, and she thanked me for looking after her son. It was during this time that Michael revealed to me that he was attracted to men, and this was something that he struggled with, constantly. I did not take his willingness to be open with me for granted. I treasured the relationship we had and the confidence he had in me; after all, he was now trying to live a life of virtue now. I wasn't judging anyone because it's my opinion that all artificial lights such as alcohol, drugs, overeating, adultery, gambling or stealing are taking someone's life. As I explained to Michael, there are seducing spirits that are in the world, and we know the word seduce means "to persuade or attempt to do evil, to lead astray, to engage or illicit sexual intercourse" according to Encarta Dictionary.

"Now the spirit speaketh expressly that in the later times, some shall depart from the faith, giving heed to seducing spirits and doctrines of devils"(1 Timothy 4:1). I told Michael that Satan is real, and he has spirits that seduce us all in different ways. Satan's job is to try and take us away from the kingdom of God; he wants us to spend an eternity in Hell where he can have company. I asked him to think of temptation as a visitor coming to your mind and knocking on the door. We can either let it in or decide not to answer.

We either have bright light or darkness bidding for our immortal soul. I explained that God has made him a male factor and he shouldn't answer to seduction. It's just like a woman trying to get the attention of a married man, begging and dressing provocatively. This happens spiritually and unseen spirits enter our thoughts. Michael looked at me in shock and told me that no one had ever explained it to him that way.

Everyone in the church has a past. We have all been slaves to sin and have given in to seducing spirits at one time or another in our lives. The bible says in 1 Cor. 6:9-11, "...Be not deceived: neither fornicators, nor idolaters, nor adulterers, nor effeminate...[for] such were some of you: but ye are washed, but ye are sanctified, but ye are justified in the name of the Lord Jesus, and by the Spirit of God." Satan is a seducing spirit; he likes to pull us away from Christ and make us void and dark.

Michael continued attending bible study until he informed us he was moving back to New York with his mother. The last time I saw him he told me to make sure I write him. After he moved, I called and spoke with him a couple of times, but he insisted that I write him. I called a few more times and could not get ahold of him. I contacted his minister and asked for his mother's number. When I spoke with his mother, she told me that Michael passed away peacefully and had spoken of me and my family until he couldn't speak anymore. She also admitted that he died in a right place with God and was not afraid, but had joy in his heart. I do realize that this level of virtue is not popular. I'm just sharing a true story of my friend Michael whom I love and miss. Hey Michael, I *finally wrote you!*

When I was a young, I successfully graduated and landed a job as a phlebotomist. I was on top of the world! I had my own apartment and was making thirteen dollars an hour (for me-that was good money). I was feeling very accomplished until I entered my apartment and flipped on the light switch. Nothing happened. I went from feeling very accomplished to feeling like a rug. No electricity meant the food would go bad, and there would be no heat.

I went to visit Miss Cleo, my neighbor, who lived directly across from me. She was about five foot five with a head full of hair. I knocked on the door, but she didn't answer right away. I was about to go back to my dark apartment- why I felt the need to share the news of my interrupted services, I don't know. Just as I stepped back inside, she opened the door. "My lights are out, and I don't get paid until next Friday," I told her.

At first she seemed to be completely ignoring me, then she asked if I had an extension cord. I thought, she's not paying me any attention, but if she needs it I'll get it. It took me a few minutes to locate it in the dark. She went back inside her apartment until I returned with the extension cord. She took the extension cord she had and plugged it into my extension cord. She plugged her end into her wall and told me to plug my end in my wall. Just like that, I had light. I will never forget her for extending the physical light that she had to me.

When you meet people whose spiritual lights are out, marriage problems, health problems, financial problems, whatever the darkness that is trying to keep them in, extend yourself and become a light for that person. "I find then a law, that, when I would do good, evil is present with me. For I delight in the law of God after the inward man...warring against the law of my mind, and bringing me into captivity to the law of sin which is in my members...O wretched man that I am! Who shall deliver me from the body of this death? I thank God through Jesus Christ our Lord!" (Rom. 7: 21-25). Being thankful is something that will help your light shine. If you live a life of selfishness, jealousy, and the like, then these things will inevitably interrupt your services. The time to shine your light is in moments of darkness, and I believe that is why we are here, to be a guiding light for others to follow. Don't extinguish someone else's light, and don't allow another person or a particular situation to extinguish your light.

Virtue—Purple

Virtue (purple) has to be added to our lives and helps us to do the right thing in the eyes of the Lord. You may not realize it, but there is a war going on for your soul. God won the victory but you have to stay on his side to *have the victory; your soul is the most valuable commodity in the world- you don't get another one. Turn the lights on. Do you realize that in heaven we will be with God and his son Jesus Christ? Heaven has the brightest light.*

Here is my prayer for you:

The Lord is my brightness of light. When darkness camped out around my spirit thou light never flicked the darker my midnight; the blinding light which helps me see oh Lord, give me your light so I may give it to others. Help me to dispel the darkness and light travels into this universe help me to follow your path. Let every attribute of darkness be incomparable. Never blot out my candlestick.

Chapter 3

Knowledge

Yellow

Yellow is a color that symbolizes the mind and intellect. Being the lightest hue in the rainbow, it is illuminating and uplifting. It inspires original thought, inquisitiveness, and creativity from the mental aspect; It is the color of new ideas. Knowledge is enlightenment.

When my daughter Hellen was younger, she met a girl named Adrienne (known as Acey for short). She immediately became part of our family; some people even thought she was my child. She had skin like onyx, richly dark, and hair like a sheep's fur, thick and wavy. Her eyes always told a story, filled with confidence, intelligence, and love. I was given the special gift of being her caregiver. I nurtured her as she grew and I later became her nurse. Hellen and Acey were inseparable; they became the best of friends.

One day, Acey's mom asked me to go to a doctor's appointment with them. I thought it was a little strange for her to ask me to go if her husband was going to be there. *Why would she need me? Nonetheless, I agreed to go with them. When the doctor came into the room, he revealed that Acey had been diagnosed with Osteosarcoma, a bone cancer. As tears streamed down her face, I asked Acey one thing, "Do you trust God?" She cried and cried, but I kept asking her the same question over and over again. I explained that this was her walk and no one else's; not her mom's or her dad's, but her walk with God. I remember praying and staying with her. About 45 minutes later she looked at me and said, "I trust God." She dried her tears, held her head up high, and decided to carry herself with dignity the whole journey through. She did it through the pain and through her amputation; she learned to drive and to date again. I never heard her complain, even though she was constantly in and out of the hospital. "I can do all things through Christ which strengtheneth me" (Phi. 4:13).*

One Sunday, during Christmas time, I was in church and someone tapped me on my shoulder. When I looked behind me, no one was there. It happened to me two more times (I know they probably thought I was crazy!). Suddenly I realized that Acey and her mom were not at church. I told my husband that I needed to leave and go check on them. I left church, went to their home, and knocked on the door. When her mom answered the door, I couldn't explain to her why I was there because I wasn't really sure myself. I went to Acey, asked her what she wanted to eat, and what gifts she wanted for Christmas. We ended up spending Christmas Eve together, and then I spent Christmas with my family.

Since school was out, my daughter asked if she could spend the night at Acey's house. I wrestled with this idea because I knew that there was a possibility that Acey might not make it through the night. However, I also knew how important this time of fellowship was for my daughter, and I did not want to rob her of this moment. I felt though, that she didn't understand that I was a mother trying to protect her daughter. Ultimately, my decision was based on pure love- a child's love for her best friend and the understanding of what true friendship means. I wanted Hellen to understand that friendship is important and being there for someone in their darkest moment is what life is all about.

I volunteered to help watch over and care for Acey until her mother returned from work. I enjoyed being in her company, as she enjoyed being in mine. One night, her mother called me and told me that Acey wanted me to help her feet touch the floor again. I felt like she got her wings and chose me to witness it; to see her off to Abraham's bosom. I did not understand. My mind couldn't comprehend what she was asking me to do. I asked her mother what she meant; she told me, "I am just telling you what she said."

I was still confused. I had just left their house and I couldn't go back because I didn't have my car. My husband had his monster truck, but I wasn't comfortable driving his truck because it was so big. I still regret not going back to see her for the last time. To this day, I am not sure if I *have ever forgiven myself. I have lamented so much about this portion of the book that tears are flowing from my eyes as I recall this particular night.*

For nine years, I have been asking myself, what did Acey mean when she asked me to help her feet touch the ground? Had she begun to feel herself fly away into the spiritual realm? Did she want me to help her face the reality that she was losing her life? Was she wanting to feel the ground beneath her feet for the very last time? I am still uncertain. What I know for sure is one day we all will move from this reality to another. Acey passed away that night. Her body lay limp in her bed. Her family, friends, and brothers & sisters in Christ were all assembled to mourn this significant loss.

After a while, the undertaker pulled into the driveway to remove Acey's body. Her parents stood weeping, and after all were able to say goodbye, I remember telling her mother, *"It's time to let her go."*

On November 3, 2017, I stood in row fifteen, at headstone six-hundred and thirty. I asked Acey for forgiveness for not helping her when she had asked. I am certain she forgave me, but I know she has her reward in Abraham's bosom. The question, however, still remains: How can I help *your feet touch the ground?*

After Acey passed, Hellen told me that she wanted to see her one more time. I told her to pray, and I did too, knowing it was an impossible task. When Hellen went to school, she was sitting at the lunch table with another friend when a young lady walked up to her and asked if she could help her find her classroom. As they walked to class, the girl told Hellen that she was new to the school. When asked her name, the girl told her Cherrelle Wilson. (Acey's middle name was Cherrelle; her older sister's last name was Wilson). After she helped Cherrelle to her class, Hellen returned to the lunch table where her friend was. Not wanting to state the obvious, she looked at her friend and before she could say anything, her friend said, "I know, she looks like Acey."

A few days later, Hellen was in creative writing class writing a paper about Acey, when her phone rang. When she looked at the phone to see who it was, the caller ID said it was from Acey! She answered it nervously, and as she said, *"hello,"* the sound of static *came through the telephone; no one said anything. This same thing occurred on two separate occasions.*

A week later, while attending a track meet, Hellen went to the restroom. She saw a girl come out of the stall and thought she knew her somehow. When the girl turned around, Hellen noticed she was wearing a backpack with a white teddy bear sticking out- the same kind of teddy bear that was put on Acey's grave! When Hellen turned to look at the girl again, she was gone. *"Be not forgetful to entertain strangers: for thereby some have entertained angels unaware" (Hebrews 13:2).*

My best friend, originally from Jamaica, was going through some transitions in her life. At the time she was unemployed, and had children to take care of while her husband was away. She had recently moved from another state and had no place to live. I spoke with my husband about her situation, and we both agreed that she could stay in our home for a little while. After she moved in, she continued her search for a job. During our conversations, I always tried to remind her that God has something better for her. I advised her to just keep it simple, stay faithful to God, and keep him first.

Days passed and no one called her for an interview, then one Sunday morning something surprising happened. Before worship began, a woman walked in wearing a cowboy hat; she stuck out like a sore thumb. I noticed that she had a light glowing around her; she just smiled at everyone and sat down to hear the sermon. The sermon was titled, *"Seek Ye First the Kingdom of God and All These Things Will Be Added unto You,"* referring to Matthew 6:33.

When worship service was over, I stood up to go shake the visitor's hand; as I walked over, an older lady almost fell. I grabbed her and asked if she was okay, holding her until she got her balance. I continued to walk over to greet the visitor, but she was gone. After Sunday dinner, the phone rang. It was the minister. It turned out that the older lady who fell on me earlier was given a large sum of money by the visitor, who whispered in her ear, *"Give the money to someone who really needed it." In one week, my best friend not only received the money, but also got three job interviews."...So shall my word be that goeth forth out of my mouth: it shall not return unto me void, but it shall accomplish that which I please, and it shall prosper in the thing whereto I sent it... For ye shall go out with joy, and be led forth with peace..." (Isaiah 55: 11-12).*

God made what seemed to be impossible possible, and moved mountains in my best friend's life. I felt like my life coincided with hers. I often think about the old woman; what seemed like a moment of weakness, turned out to be a momentous occasion. She was given the responsibility to help someone! In situations like this, we are baffled at the amazing things God will do.

As we add knowledge (yellow) into our lives, let us remember the old spiritual hymn that tells us, "we will understand it better, by and by." "For now we see through a glass, darkly; but then face to face: now I know in part; but then shall I know even as also I am known" (1 Cor. 12:12).

Chapter 4

Temperance

Green

Green is the most common color in nature. We think of it as a balanced, healthy and youthful color. It represents spring and rebirth, as well as prosperity and self-restraint. There are things in life that you may want to indulge in, things that may be plenteous around you, but you have to renew your thinking like a caterpillar's metamorphosis into a butterfly. Soar above common troubles in life.

Growing up, I learned that if your job is to sweep floors, you should have the attitude to be the best floor sweeper you can be. So, I carried that mindset on the job. Many years ago, I worked at a restaurant with an all female staff. During this time I was a cashier and was awarded employee of the month. Jealousy began to rear its ugly head. My coworkers fussed at me for leaving my station and accused me when money came up short in the register. My car was keyed, and one of my coworkers hit me and pretended like it was an accident. After that she followed me around the store like clockwork and ultimately got my boss involved. She told him that I wasn't doing my job, and that I was fraternizing and flirting with multiple men who patronized the restaurant. Truthfully, she was the real culprit. My coworker and I had three meetings with the boss, and each time she would lie to him about me and would get my other coworkers involved.

Whew! My temperance was getting a workout! I remember being hurt, upset, and saddened by the way they were treating me. *"Be ye angry, and sin not: let not the sun go down upon your wrath"* (Ephesians 4:26). I did-

n't want to misrepresent God but I thought to myself, enough is enough. I prayed to God and asked him to help me resist responding to the harassment in a negative way because ultimately, what God thought of me was more important than what my coworkers thought of me. They took turns talking to my boss and lying about me until my manager said, "OK. Now, what do you have to say about these allegations?"

Anger and temperance wrestled with my mind, and through the tears I opened my mouth and tried to talk. Nothing would come out, so I tried again. It wasn't until the second try that I realized I was having an asthma attack. All I could do was motion for help. The coworker who initiated this stressful situation was the first to take action and call 9-1-1, she recognized the signs because she also suffered from asthma.

The ambulance came and took me to the hospital. The doctor stabilized me by giving me a breathing treatment, and calmed me down by explaining that this attack was brought on by stress. I decided that from then on, I would never let Satan and his demons upset me like that again. *"...let every man be swift to hear, slow to speak, slow to wrath: For the wrath of man worketh not the righteousness of God?" (James 1:19-20).*

Six months later, I was doing some housework when my phone rang; my friend asked if I had seen the front page of the newspaper. I told her I hadn't and she told me that it was about my coworker. One of the married men that she flirted with was accused of burning down his home. His lawyer said he was innocent because he was with my coworker at work. However, because of the negative publicity, she was fired from the restaurant. Shortly after this situation, my husband was called into the ministry. I am so glad I was able to use temperance (green) because without it, my Christian role as the minister's wife may not have been taken seriously.

Chapter 5

Patience

Blue

The color blue is the same as the sky and the sea. It is often associated with depth and stability. It also represents trust, loyalty, wisdom, healing, confidence, intelligence, faith, truth, and heaven. Through patience, we possess our souls. "For what shall it profit a man, if he shall gain the whole world, and lose his own soul?" (Mark 8:36) As the songwriter Albert Edward Brumley wrote in the song *This World is Not My Home*, "Oh Lord, you know, I have no friend like you. If heaven's not my home, then Lord what will I do?"

One year my best friend and I signed up for a ladies retreat. We all met at the church in different shifts, according to the assignment: leaders and speakers, decorators and food preparers, and travelers. The first shift that met was decorators and food preparers, second shift was the leaders and speakers, and third shift was people like me, fill-ins. I chose the late crew because I got off work late and needed some time to catch my breath.

We finally pulled up to the campground where the retreat was being held. As we got closer we noticed a lot of the women were crying. My best friend kept telling me, "Something has happened." Once we parked and got out of the car, I asked one of the sister's what happened. She told me that one of the elder's wives, my friend, had died. She was putting a table-cloth on one of the tables when she collapsed. The ambulance came, but it was too late- she'd had a heart attack and was pronounced dead on arrival. Surprised by the news I said, "No she didn't." It was at that moment I realized she had no reason to lie to me. I immediately exercised patience in this stressful situation. I remember telling myself to be strong- not only for me, but for the other sisters as well. I embraced the sister and my best friend, still in disbelief and firmly held their hands in this time of sorrow. Soon, all the ladies were circled together praying and comforting one another. My friend, who had passed was an elder's wife, a part of my circle of friends, and church family. Her husband was a football player at for Alabama State University and he went on to play professional football for the Kansas City Chiefs. She was responsible for my son taking singing lessons, and she helped raise money for him to go to college. She took me to my doctor's visit when I broke my leg in six places, and I could not walk. She also took me to my physical therapy.

I thought back to the month before at our Valentine's Day dinner, she arrived late. I was already at the table seated next to someone, and had saved a seat for my husband; I thought it would be rude to go and sit at her table, so I stayed where I was. Whenever a speaker would tell a joke or make a good point, she would turn her body completely around, to the point of discomfort, and look at me and smile. Looking back now, I believe it was her making a special effort to say goodbye.

I looked around the campground. My grief and shock would have to wait. "My brethren, count it all joy when ye fall into divers temptations; Knowing *this, that the trying of your faith worketh patience.*"(James 1:2-3)

As the minister and the leaders of the church were arriving, I told the program director that if she needed me, I would be willing to fill in because there were many sisters who wanted to cancel the retreat. The leader told me that we would go on with the program.

All of a sudden, about twenty bats (that's right- I said bats) came flying down from the ceiling. We had been going to this campground for years and had never encountered an incident like this! Everyone was in shock, ducking, dodging, and even lying on the floor! A group of men, who were part of a Boy Scout group, heard us singing songs of Zion and yelled to us to turn off the lights and be quiet, so the bats would come out on their own. Okay, wait. My sister and my friend fell asleep serving the Lord while there were twenty bats flying around our heads in the dark?

I was calm until I felt something around my feet. I slowly looked down and a voice said, "Hi Auntie!" I was thankful that I didn't pack up and leave or run off screaming. I thought there was a bat on my feet, but I quickly realized it was my niece so I calmed down. The bats eventually left and as everyone regrouped; the program director told me that she needed me. *"But let patience have her perfect work..."* (James 1:4). *As we continued with the program, I was called to say a prayer. In my heart I knew she would want us to carry on with the program.*

I was wearing blue and although I didn't remember the prayer, I remembered the essence of it. I recited the theme of Christian women; coming together for the purpose of healing, and that is what we were going to do in Christ Jesus' name. If we are Christians, then we are to be mature. If we are going to be with the Lord, then we have to change first by taking off mortality and putting on immortality, because we need each other. It was at this time that God's presence began to fill the room. I have been to many retreats geared towards women and Christian empowerment, but never had I experienced anything, until this retreat; it was so candid and naked. We continued to encourage and lift each other up throughout the evening. Later we retired to our assigned cabin for the night.

The next morning was filled with anticipation. As we ate breakfast, a few women spoke to those who were separated, widowed or divorced from their husbands. One sister spoke about how she separated from her husband and how he died during that separation. She told us about his sickness and how she took over as his caretaker even though they were separated. She said that he became a whore when he got sick, and through all that happened, she still didn't go anywhere. I believe that she was using patience. Although she was under stress, she was waiting for God and was not complaining. She was talking to God through prayer and more importantly, she was listening to him when he spoke to her. "Ye are the light of the world. A city that is set on an hill cannot be hid" (Matthew 5:14). Whatever struggles you are going through that try your patience, know that patience is an important attribute you need to make it in this world. "[For] In your patience possess ye your souls" (Luke 21:19).

Chapter 6

Godliness

Indigo

Indigo is a color that represents "wisdom, self-mystery, intuition and spiritual realization" (colorpsychology.org). It symbolizes godliness, which "[conforms] to the laws and wishes of God" (dictionary.com). Exodus 20:1-3 says, "And God spake all these words, saying, I am the LORD thy God which have brought thee out of the house of bondage. Thou shalt have no other gods before me." God is a jealous god; he reminds us how he delivered us, and metaphorically how we have been brought out of Egypt, the wilderness, slavery, and sin. God has proven that he is the one true God. If we want to please God, we have to get into his mind and carry that mindset with us. Jeremiah says, "They have built also the high places of Ba'-al, to burn their sons with fire *for burnt offerings unto Ba'-al, which I commanded not, nor spake it, neither came it into my mind"(Jeremiah 19:5). A lot of people are worshipping God, according to what they think is right.*

God never needs to have a 'Plan B'. He knows what is going to happen when it's going to happen; it's all in his plan. Before time began, God held a meeting to determine the counsel - God the Father, the Son, and the Holy Spirit. From the time that God first breathed into the nostrils of man until Jesus Christ hung, bled, and died on the cross was four hundred years. "...one day is with the Lord as a thousand years, and a thousand years as one day" (2 Peter 3:8). When Satan thought that he had stopped God's plan of killing Jesus Christ on the cross, Christ purchased the church with his own blood; meaning, he tore down the "middle wall of partition" (Ephesians 2:14), giving **everyone** access to the church, which is the bride of Christ. God's has a very simple plan for everyone to follow. In order to access his kingdom, you have to *hear the word of God (Romans 10:17); you have to believe that what he says is true (Mark 16:16); you also need to repent of our sins [past and present](Luke 13:3), confess that Jesus Christ is the Son of God (Romans 10:10), and finally be baptized for the remission of your sins (Galatians 3:27). Following these steps places you into God's family forever and voila- you become a light!*

Growing up, I would often spend the night with different relatives. I had an aunt, who was a Jehovah's Witness, a cousin who was Seventh Day Adventist, a grandmother who was Baptist, and another who belonged to the AME church. My half-sister was Muslim, and both my mother and godparents were members of the Church of God in Christ. As a twenty one year old young lady, I could not understand why peoples' religion had to be so different; everyone said it didn't matter how you worshipped God. I began to think about this and would ask myself, *"Is there a God? Do I believe in the bible?"* The *answer for me was yes. "For what shall it profit a man, if he shall gain the whole world, and lose his own soul?"* (Mark 8:36). There is a God and there is a par*ticular way that he wants to be worshipped. God wants an intimate relationship with each one of us. Satan is always busy. "…your adversary the devil, as a roaring lion, walketh about, seeking whom he may devour…"* (1 Peter 5:8). God *gives us a choice. "…choose you this day whom ye will serve…"* (Joshua 24:15).

Satan wants to take God's worship; he says in Isaiah 14:13-14 "I will ascend into heaven, I will exalt my throne above the stars of God: I will sit also upon the mount of the congregation...I will ascend above the heights of the clouds; I will be like the most High." We have to make sure that we are not worshipping Satan or false gods. Just as Satan tried to tempt Jesus on the mountain, he will try and do the same to us. He is an imitator and a tempter. He has come to steal, kill, and destroy us. You must not let darkness have rule over your life. We have to fight against the "wiles of the devil" (Ephesians 6:11), we have to fight to let there be light. The bible tells us to seek, ask, and knock. When you hear the truth, you *will know it as the truth.*

There is a story from the bible about a young man named Joseph. He was the second youngest of twelve brothers. Joseph's father, Jacob, loved and favored him; he presented him with a coat of many colors. Joseph had a dream one night, and the next day he went and told his brothers about the dream. By this time, Joseph's brothers had become jealous of him; when they saw him coming, they plotted against him and threw him in a pit. They would have killed him, but his brother Reuben stopped them, suggesting they sell him instead. So, they sold Joseph and he ended up in Potiphar's house (an officer of Pharaoh). Potiphar saw that God was with Joseph and put him in control of everything he had. That is, until Satan got ahold of Potiphar's wife. She tried to seduce Joseph to sleep with her and when Joseph refused, she lied and had him thrown into prison. He stayed in prison until Pharaoh had a dream that no one, except Joseph, could interpret.

There were seven years of famine after Joseph was released from prison. The famine was so severe, that his family had to travel to Egypt for food. Joseph's brothers had to come to him after all, and because he had the spirit of God in him, he was able to have a divine spirit of forgiveness in him as well. God "was with Joseph" (Genesis 39:2), and he knew that Joseph would not sin against him. He was promoted to second in command during that time, standing by Pharaoh's side. Pharaoh asked his servant, "Can we find such a one as this is, a man in whom the Spirit of God is?" (Genesis 41:38). Pharaoh recognized the God of Joseph, and all of Egypt was told about the one true God because of him.

We have a heavenly father who loves us. You may have brothers like Joseph who betray you. Zechariah 13:6 says that "...Those with which I was wounded in the house of my friends." We will be sold or asked to sell our souls. There will be people who are jealous of you, and people who lie on you and try to put down your goals and dreams. God *will* "...*make [your] enemies [your] footstool*" (Luke 20:43).

Christ has come that we may have life, the ability to move and breathe, and to give and receive light. Your light must keep the candle burning, unwavered by the winds of the liar.

Godliness—Indigo

There are times when you will feel over-whelmed and will want to stop trying and give up, but God's spirit is moving. If you are a Christian, you should notice that the evil one calls evil good and good evil. Instead of giving or receiving the light, there are those who want to bring you down. Extend the cord from your power source and open your eyes. Godliness (indigo) is another important attribute to have in your life because we have to be able to practice what we preach. 1 Tim. 4:8 says, "For bodily exercise profiteth little: but godliness is profitable unto all things, having promise of the life that now is, and of that which is to come."

Chapter 7

Brotherly Kindness

Orange

Orange combines the energy of red and the happiness of yellow. It is associated with joy, sunshine, and the tropics. Orange symbolizes enthusiasm, fascination, happiness, creativity, determination, attraction, success, encouragement, and stimulation. "Brotherly love is the love for one's fellow-man as a brother. The expression is taken from the Greek word Philadelphia, which [was] a trait distinguished in Early Christian communities" (Wikipedia).

I first learned about brotherly kindness as a child. I was the oldest of two brothers and five first cousins. When the sound of the ice cream truck came through my neighborhood, we would run to the truck with excitement. Most of my cousins and brothers would have little to no money, but my grandfather would always slip me a little more money. No one knew that I had extra money, but I felt a sense of responsibility or brotherly kindness to ensure that everyone left the ice cream truck with *something*. *I still think of the ice cream truck when people ask me about the issues of life today: politics, crime rate, racial divide, trust of law enforcement, financial instability, etc. Brotherly love is missing today. During my childhood, there was a sense of pride in your neighborhood, your community, and your country. We didn't need to worry about what was on television before 9 o'clock, like the sex and violence that children are privy to now. We could leave our key under the doormat, and know that it would still be there when we got home. It seems like everything that was locked down has been loosed. There are loose morals and selfishness. I'm asking everyone who is reading this book to find your passion (women causes, chil-*

dren concerns, feeding the hungry, defending the country, or even debating gun laws) because brotherly love is needed today more than ever.

Brotherly love is the only reason why some children in this country are not homeless, and why someone was able to eat dinner tonight. Someone you know might be without transportation; look around and get out of your self-love or selfishness and help someone. I know there are people with big hearts who are waiting for a sign. What exactly are you waiting for? There are mothers, married or single, who need your help with their children, or a minister who voluntarily starts a small congregation with no expectations of getting a paycheck that could use your support.

I believe that if there are any prejudice people in the world, they should work with infants of different nationalities. If you are willing to hate little children because of their race, then there is no light in you. Once there was a little girl who asked me why my hands were dirty. I knew she was taught this at home, but in spite of it I loved her as I love my own grandchildren. On a field trip, there was another little girl who asked me why my skin was different than hers. I told her it was because my mother and grandmother's skin was like this. She told me she wanted skin like mine, and I told her that she should be happy with the skin she's in because it is beautiful. She replied with, "Oh, I got it!" We should all be thankful for whom God made us and appreciate others for who they are.

I'm reminded of a story in Luke 16:4 about a

beggar named Lazarus who begged outside of a rich man's gate. Lazarus died and went into Abraham's bosom; the rich man died and opened his eyes in Hell. The rich man asked Lazarus if he could dip the tip of his finger in water and touch his tongue so that he may get relief. The rich man wanted to go to his father's house to tell his brethren not to come to this place of torment because Hell was not a place for them to come. He wanted to have brotherly kindness, but it was too late for him. I'm begging you, as Lazarus begged the rich man, to show brotherly kindness to your fellow man.

Christians have a badge of love; we have brothers and sisters in Christ whom we can rely on. If you are a leader, you need to model brotherly kindness to those that are following your path. It takes more courage to keep loving and shining when you're facing hate most of the time. I want to ignite a light in each of you to understand that you can show brotherly love and assist those in need. What kind of world would it be if we were to show more brotherly love (orange)?

Chapter 8

Unconditional Love & Nurturing

—◆————————◆—

Pink

The color pink is symbolic of unconditional love and nurturing.

A young man I used to know, named Derrick, received a full-ride scholarship to Yale University. His parents were so proud of him, and bragged about him to everyone who listened. Shortly before school started, Derrick found out that he was going to be a father. In order to help take care of his new family, Derrick enlisted into the Army. Derrick tried to call his mother and father every Sunday, but his sister would quietly tell him that they did not want to speak to him. Twenty years later, Derrick still tries to call and speak to his parents every Sunday. His sister told him that his parents didn't even want him to attend their funerals. Isn't that sad? Sure, his parents were disappointed that he lost his scholarship to Yale, but why would they turn that disappointment into something so cruel. It's okay to feel disappointed for a little while, but please, don't lose your soul harboring such coldness in your heart. Forgiveness and love are very important.

Love is something that we all have to work on. How can we show brotherly love for someone who has ill will towards you? Practice patience and prayer-carry out good will; even though it will feel like you are swimming against the current, keep on swimming. It's like lifting a heavy object or doing a vigorous exercise, those things profit little compared to what our God can do, Godly exercise profits much. If you want love in your life, you have to bench press hatred, various injustices, and even unforgiving spirits. We as human beings will never have a happy and colorful life if

we can't forgive. There needs to be a lot of weight lifting; forgive yourself. People who have not forgiven
themselves have a very hard time forgiving and loving
others. "And be ye kind one to another, tenderhearted,
forgiving one another, even as God for Christ's sake
hath forgiven you" (Eph. 4:32).

As a child my baby brother was picked on and
called an albino because of the color of his skin. When I
was about eight years old, a set of twins taunted him
saying that they were going to beat him up. My cousin
was going to help me retaliate against them because I
could not let them do that to my brother. When I got
ready to fight, I looked up and my cousin was jumping
up and down cheering me on, shouting at me to get
them. I loved my brother so much that I got into a
physical fight. I could have gotten hurt but love didn't
care.

God loved the world so much that he gave his
only begotten son to this dark place, so that we could
have a chance of everlasting life. It is for this cause that
I believe that no one should have self-esteem problems.
Think about it; your soul is worth more than the whole
world to God and he owns everything. You are consid-
ered the most valuable asset; those of us that are Christians don't belong to ourselves. We are the property of
God; we were purchased by the blood of Jesus. Yes- we
were bought with a price and have been translated
from the darkness into the light (1 Cor. 6:20, 7:23). You
may be wondering, *why are you talking about Jesus and
the love of God? It's simple. It is the purest form of love and
support you can ever get.*

Be mindful that although you may not see God physically, know that when you inhale and exhale without the help of any machines you are blessed. The Earth is approximately 92,955,807 miles from the sun (https://www.space.com/17081-how-far-is-earth-from-the-sun.html). As powerful as the sun's rays are, God placed the Earth exactly where it needed to be so we can live, breathe, and walk the Earth freely instead of burning up. We may take a day off but God never takes a day off. God allows us to wake up every day and be in good health. Everything may not be the way you would like it to be, but guess what? You are here for a reason. A smile can brighten someone's day easily when greeting someone who may be having a bad day. A simple, "I love you" could mean the world to someone who doesn't hear that as often.

In Joshua 1:6-27, Joshua fought the battle of Jericho, and love brought the walls down. For six days, God ordered the Israelites to march around the city so their enemies could surrender. "And seven priests shall bear before the ark seven trumpets of rams' horns: and the seventh day ye shall compass the city seven times, and the priests shall blow with the trumpets" (Jos. 6:4). When the trumpets were blown, "...the people shall shout with a great shout: and the wall of the city shall fall down flat..." (Jos. 6:5). The Israelites obeyed God and that is why God allowed them to be victorious. God also allowed Rahab the harlot and her family to be saved because she hid the messengers. Joshua 6:25 says, "And Joshua saved Rahab the harlot alive, and her father's household and all that she had; and she dwelleth in Israel even unto this day; because she hid the messengers, which Joshua sent to spy out Jericho." You have to be careful when dealing with the children of God. Don't mistreat or misuse God's people, if God be for you, no one can be against you. Vengeance belongs to God.

The story of Rahab reminds me of the story of Esther and how she was able to save an entire nation of people. King Ahasuerus was married to a rebellious woman, and sought to find a humble and submissive wife, he chose Esther because of her humble spirit. Soon after Esther became queen, a man named Haman devised a plot to kill all the Jews. Her uncle, Mordecai, sent word to Esther that this was a time to speak up and plead to her husband, the king, to save their lives. She asked her uncle as well as her chambermaids, to fast and pray so that the Lord would deliver them from the wicked hands of Haman (Est. 4: 6-16). Whenever we go through trials, we should always pray to get us through.

Haman hated Mordecai because he wouldn't bow down to him, so in return Haman built gallows to kill Mordecai (Est. 3:5, 14). Esther went and told the King about Haman's plot and saved her uncle and all of the Jews. She showed unconditional love for her uncle and for her nation of people when she said, "...if I perish, I perish" (Est. 4:16). Learn to have an ear for wisdom. God used Esther to save her nation (Est. 7-8) . Be careful when you are digging ditches for other people. When you are plotting evil against someone- the evil may turn back on you. I don't want to be used by Satan.

I was on my way to work one day, and when I got to the gate I realized that I had forgotten my CAC card, a card that allows me access to the military post. I looked in the glovebox, my purse, my trunk.

The soldier asked, *"Ma'am is there a problem?"*

I responded, *"Yes, I seemed to have misplaced my CAC card."*

He said, *"Well, you have to go to the trailer and get a temporary pass."*

I went to the trailer, showed them my license, and they gave me a temporary pass for one day. I asked if I could have a frequent pass, since I worked there. The guy said no, I would have to either get a new CAC card or get another one day pass. Once I got back on post, I mused over the fact that one day I'm going to have to be somewhere more important than this job. Sometimes, we become misplaced and lose our way, and are unaware of where we are until we are presented with a situation that denies us access to where we need to be.

When I lay all my talents and compassion down, I will shed the temporary flesh and put on the everlasting spirit. I know now that I don't want gate trouble, I want an automatic entrance. Back at the gate, I thought, God let me have the right pass to get into heaven so please let me hear the most sacred sound, *"...'Well done good and faithful servant...'"* (Matt. 25:21). *My deep-*

est purpose and truest intent in this book is to evoke in myself and others to live as a "...good and faithful servant..." (Matt. 25:21).

Never forget the fact that this isn't heaven, but neither is it hell. I don't care if you are a king in a palace reigning over your territory, or a peasant poor and needy- it's still not heaven because it's going to be better than anything here on Earth or anything that you can imagine. There will be no thoughts, no misunderstandings, no worries, and thank God *no tears. The thing that sends shivers down my spine is the fact that people think that it's okay if they go to hell; they say that it's okay because they won't be by themselves. This is nothing to joke about. It will be a very torturous situation with tremendous pain and suffering every second of every day. I want to encourage you not to go to hell. "For a day in thy courts is better than a thousand. I had rather be a doorkeeper in the house of God, than to dwell in the tents of wickedness" (Psa. 84:10).*

I once spoke with a woman named Delta. I met her at church one Sunday morning while she was visiting our church. She asked for prayer because she was scheduled to have a routine surgery in the next few days. But, before I knew this information, I was compelled to speak to her about investing herself in heaven. I remember walking and talking with her about the steps to salvation. She told me that she didn't want to become a member of the church, because she was going to have to deal with recovery after her surgery and didn't want to be a burden to church.

A few days after her surgery, Delta crossed my mind and I began asking those that knew her how she was doing. I was told that shortly after her surgery she was placed in ICU and was currently fighting for her life. Again I was compelled to see her. When I got to the ICU, the nurse greeted me and asked if she could help me. I told her that I had come to see Delta, but the nurse told me that only immediate family was allowed. I explained that I was the minister's wife from her church, and I just wanted to pray for her. The nurse told me to give her 10 mins and she would allow me to see Delta. Before this, I remember standing at the door peeking through the window. I had an urgency to see her and know how she was doing. A week had already passed by since we last spoke. I felt like I was having a deja vu moment, as I remembered what had taken place at the church. I wondered if in her state, she would get to live another day. I waited about another thirty minutes to see her, and just as I was about to give up and go home, the nurse came to me and said I could finally see her.

She was hooked up to a lot of machines and had tubes and cords everywhere. When she saw me, she jumped up out of the bed. She started gesturing- trying to talk to me, but I could not understand anything that she was saying. All the equipment started going off. The nurses came in and tried to calm her down and get her back in the bed. I was afraid the nurses were going to make me leave, but thankfully they didn't. After she calmed down, I went to God in heaven on her behalf.

I prayed with her and then I left. She was later transferred to another hospital where she recovered. After her recovery, she came back to church, got baptized, and gave her life to the Lord. One day, she told me her account of what happened in the ICU room the day I visited her. According to her, when I walked into her ICU room, she saw a dark shadow on the other side of the room slowly moving towards her. She knew that her life was not in order, but she felt like the dark shadow was death. She said she saw herself in a field with her mother, who had passed. When she woke up, she gestured to me and tried speaking to me to tell me about the shadow. However, once I started praying for her, she saw the shadow move back and fade into the darkness. God's Love & Light overcame the darkness.

We often feel as if we have an enormous amount time to do everything. We should know by now death comes like a thief in the night. No one knows when their time on earth is up. For Delta, the surgery was supposed to be a routine procedure. Through the worst of what happened to her, God was merciful and gracious enough to give her another chance at life. She could have left this world with no chance of becoming a Christian and learning more about God, his will, and his word. But the unconditional love that God has for us all, he showed to her and allowed her another chance to make it right; don't wait until it's too late. "Charity [love] suffereth long, *and is kind; charity envieth not; charity vaunteth not itself, is not puffed up..." (1 Cor. 13:4). Love (pink) lifted me, Love lifted me, when nothing else could help- Love lifted me.*

Chapter 9

Encountering Darkness

Black

The color black is associated with negativity. It is a mysterious color, symbolic of the unknown. "Black objects absorb all colours so no light is reflected" (https://www.sciencelearn.org.nz/resources/47-colours-of-light). Black is distinctly darkness, there is no light within it. It creates a barrier between itself and the outside world by providing comfort while protecting its emotions and feelings, hiding its vulnerabilities, insecurities and lack of self-confidence.

There are times in our lives when life seems like the air is favorable for a tornado, and just like that, we seem to have no control over it. It seems that as soon as we can predict the temperature or dew-point, unexpected hail comes down upon us. Faith goes in at these times as a seed that has to be turned or tilled in order to grow. Sow the seed and take root. "For we wrestle not against flesh and blood, but against principalities, against powers, against the rulers of the darkness of this world, against spiritual wickedness in high places" (Ephesians 6:12). It could be on your job, it could be at church, it could be in your family- don't let Satan pin you. Even if you feel like someone has dug a grave six feet deep, threw you in there, and threw dirt on top of you (and metaphorically, Jesus got up in three days, so know that you *will rise again just as the Lord did and you will be "renewed day by day" [2 Corinthians 4:16]). You may be thinking about putting yourself that far down, but find a socket and a light source, get an extra cord if you need to, and plug yourself into Jesus.*

As I mentioned in the introduction, our eyes are the windows to the soul. "The light of the body is the eye: if therefore thine eye be single, thy whole body be full of light" (Matt. 6:22). Job 24:15-16 also says, "…the eye also…waiteth for the twilight, saying, No eye shall see me: and disguiseth his face. In the dark they dig through houses, which they had marked for themselves in daytime: they know not the light." Most of the time we think of singleness as a negative thing, but here, God is telling us of one, not one of many. If you choose God, you will have a full life, because God is a consuming fire. Just as your eyes, interpret to your (eye: mind), it must remain single. It interprets what it houses, which is the singleness of mind. It works in the same way if someone is single or not taking company. There is no competition for your attention.

God deals with us as single people or individuals. Everyone around you may not have a relationship with God because you cannot serve two masters (Matt. 6:24). God wants to come in and commune with you. "Behold, I stand at the door and knock: if any man hear my voice, and open the door, I will come in to him, and will sup with him, and he with me" (Rev. 3:20).

Some of the characteristics of a lazy picker are selfishness, an unforgiving spirit, and inability to accept love, lying, and projecting denial. Projection denial is a "theory in psychology in which humans defend themselves against their own unconscious impulses or qualities by denying their existence in themselves while attributing them to others" (https://en.m.wikipedia.org/wiki/Psychological_projection). James 3:15 says, "wisdom descendeth not from above, but *is earthly, sensual, devilish." A life with the Lord is the best life to live. It seems like people aren't looking at what is right or wrong anymore, instead they are siding with what the majority decides. We must hold fast to our faith, even if we are not with the majority; we must let our Christian light shine brighter than ever in these dark days. I know that heaven is going to be worth more than any approval or status that we might receive from man. Judgment is coming. If God required your soul tonight, where would you spend eternity?*

As a Floridian and a self-proclaimed 'sunshine' girl, when I left Florida and moved farther north, I realized that I had never seen a leaf that wasn't green or brown. Most of the time everything was pretty much green. I never really experienced the seasons change in Florida. I also experienced seasonal depression and didn't realize it. When you have responsibilities you just keep going. I would go to the dollar store and pick up the brightest flowers and vase to place in the middle of the table to look at, and then it occurred to me that *this is what I'm here to do, to encourage and to brighten up a room. I believe my purpose is to spread light and brighten others' lives with the light of the word.*

One day I realized that I had been continuously cleaning straw from my window sill for the last week. I went out of town, and when I came back there was a bird's nest in my window. I cleaned it out and found a small tear in my screen. Before I could repair or replace it, a mother bird flew to the window and looked at the spot where her nest was. I knew that look because I've had it before. It's the look where you tilt your head to the side because you need clarification on something, or when you can't believe the words that are coming out of someone's mouth. Her neck tilted to the left and then to the right, back and forth and back again to the center. She then flew away and returned with another bird, like she needed a witness. I wonder if it was Mr. Cardinal.

Mrs. Cardinal then came back with straw and began rebuilding the nest. I was so impressed. Because of her faith, action, and determination, she didn't let me discourage her. "Every wise woman buildeth her house: but the foolish plucketh it down with her hands" (Proverbs 14:1). I decided that my window sill would become *her window sill (because I had an old fashioned window that pulled down and the bird was on the outside ledge); she worked very hard and nested in preparation for birth. Just like I had done for my kids and grands, I was determined to have a comfortable, clean, and safe place for them to grow and one day soar and fly away. But if for some reason the little chicks couldn't soar, mama would nudge them out of the nest and be ready to catch them between flights. As I looked out at the bird's nest, I thought of how the mama bird fed the baby chicks because they were not able to feed themselves. I would sneak them bread when the mama bird left to go get her babies some food. The bible says in Matthew 6:26, "Behold the fowls of the air: for they sow not, neither do they reap, nor gather into barns; yet your heavenly Father feedeth them. Are ye not much better than they?"*

A young man named Allen told me that his mother was a great baker, and during the holidays people got her to bake things for them. One Thanksgiving, his aunt called their house and asked him to speak to mother. She wanted to know when she would pick up her pies. Allen went to the room to wake his mother who was always hard to awaken; he shook her and went back to the telephone to tell his aunt that she wasn't waking up. He tried several more times to wake his mother, and each time he returned to tell his aunt that his mother wasn't moving. Alarmed, Allen's aunt sent a friend over to the house to check on her sister, and they saw that she had been shot. They found out later that his father had shot her nine times. While at the hospital, the doctor's saved one bullet that was lodged close to her heart. Amazingly, his mother lived a few years after the incident, and later she died from related causes. Allen's father went to jail for five years for the shooting.

What color can you look at to brighten that gloom and doom in your life? For a long time Allen had trouble forgiving his father, until he heard a gospel preacher teach on forgiveness and how God forgives us based on how we forgive others. We can't keep harboring unforgiveness. The bible tells us that God "heals the brokenhearted and binds up wounds" (Psalms 147:3). Eventually, Allen forgave his father and as a result his children and wife were able to meet their grandfather and father-in-law before he died. Allen went on to become a great husband and father. At one time, there was a dark cloud that he could have chosen, but he decided to walk in the light and choose the path of his heavenly father.

It is so strange, the things that Satan wants from us; he wanted the body of Moses (Jude 1:9), he wanted the worship of Jesus (Matt. 4:9), the prayer of Daniel (Dan. 6:13), and he wanted Job to curse God and die (Job 2:5, 9). He wants the virginity of young women, the sobriety of young men; he wanted the obedience of Adam and Eve (Gen. 3:4) and Esau's birthright (Gen. 25:31). Satan was put out of heaven, so now he wants to take away your joy. When the children of God assemble, *know that Satan will also assemble himself. But, "...the joy of the Lord is [our] strength" (Nehemiah 8:10); Satan wants to steal, kill, and destroy you. The Lord comes to build and give life more abundantly (John 10:10). Remember that we have to let there be light; not just physical light but soul, mind, and spiritual lighting also. When you go out into the world with your light on, know that all day long Satan will use people and situations to try and put your light out. You must be that bright color of faith (red), virtue (purple), knowledge (yellow), temperance (green), patience (blue), godliness (indigo), brotherly kindness (orange) and love (pink). Always remember that "...perfect love casteth out fear" (1 John 4:18).*

Chapter 10

Courage

Gold

Gold is a precious metal that is associated with illumination, love, compassion, courage, magic and wisdom. It is also associated with joy, happiness, intellect and energy (www.patheos.com). Psalm 119-127 says, "Therefore I love your commandments more than gold, yes more than fine gold." Courage is further defined as having heart, spirit, and the attitude of facing and dealing with anything recognized as dangerous, difficult or painful-instead of withdrawing from it. It is the quality of being fearless or brave and having valor.

While watching my favorite TV show, *The Andy Griffith Show, a commercial came across the screen advertising an upcoming breakfast honoring several women of courage in our community. According to the advertisement, one of the women being honored, Ann Kaggins, was a member of the Lord's church. I thought to myself, I have to go. After all, I had not seen Ann since my dear friend Gayle Jackson died. The night after the funeral, we reminisced on all the things we remembered about Gayle- about how all of our friends were moving so fast from life to death, from temporary to eternal. I remember telling her and my friend, Sarah Powell, that I was planning to write a book. I told them I wanted to try to get others to understand that in the spiritual world, there are only two paths to follow in this life: the path of lightness or the path of darkness. I thought about golden opportunities and how precious our time is on Earth. Please take the time to support good causes and celebrate others' lives and good works.*

I hurried to the Women of Courage breakfast, which began at seven o'clock in the morning. I was so happy to "rejoice with them that rejoice..." (Romans

12:15). I have noticed that sometimes in our society we do it backwards; we rejoice when people weep and weep when they rejoice. We should weep with others' when they experience misfortunes and rejoice with them during their golden opportunities. When I arrived at the breakfast, I attempted to pay for my ticket, but I learned that my name was on the VIP list and my ticket had been paid for. I felt honored. The usher told me that I would be sitting at table twenty-nine. I fixed my plate and entered a crowded room. I sat at my table located in the front row with the Who's Who of our community.

The breakfast was so beautiful, and I could not help but be transported to heaven. I thought about how glorious heaven will be because of choosing a life of light with Jesus Christ. I've had plenty of storms in my life (and I'm certain that you have too) that have caused the lights to temporarily be out, but I'm glad that Jesus is the light of my life- the light that no storm or earthquake of a situation can black out. You may be dealing with a situation right now, maybe fear or self-esteem or loneliness, it is only *temporary; the Lord will see you through. Trust in him, believe in him, and be faithful to him. When God prepares a table for you, as in the twenty-third psalms, we don't have to worry about being in the presence of our enemies (Psa. 23:5). What a glorious table that is, where the enemy can do us no harm.*

As we were seated at the table, we introduced ourselves to each other. *"My name is Sherronda Bowman,"* I said.

"Bowman?" a woman echoes. We began talking and I later discovered this woman was my husband's long lost cousin! Each day we live has golden nuggets in it.

About thirty years ago, I was visiting my mother, and she had a friend visiting her that day. She turned to me and suggested that I meet her son Sam. She picked up the telephone to call him. He came over and upon meeting me stuck out his hand and said, "*Hi, I'm Sam.*"

"*Hello,*" *I replied,* "*I'm Sherronda.*" *He asked me if he could take me out to dinner. I agreed as we got along quite well. Afterwards, Sam dropped me off at home.*

Just as I was about to go inside my neighbor told me, "*That's Sam. You're aware that he is married?*"

Confused I said, "*No, I don't think so. His mother introduced us.*"

"*Sorry...*" *she replied,* "*...but I'm positive.*"

I later found out that my neighbor was right. I couldn't understand why a mother would introduce me to her married son. I made up my mind right then that there would be no more dinners with Sam. The next evening there was a knock on my door. I looked through the peephole, it was Sam. I opened the door and explained that I could no longer see him because he was married. I expected him to say, "Okay, I understand." Or... maybe have a conversation about my uncomfortableness with the situation. I was not prepared for what happened next. Sam pulled a gun out, pointed it at me, and told me to shut up and get in the car.

I had never seen a real gun before; I was *so scared. Oh Lord he's going to kill me, I thought. As we walked in the darkness of the night, I did as I was told and got in his car. At this point, I'm crying. "Please shut up before I shoot you right now!" Sam said. Fear set into my mind, and I was physically trembling. As we rode down the street, I thought to myself open the door and jump, but he was driving like a maniac. My tears were my only comfort at that time. When the car stopped, I looked up to see that we were at the beach. "Out of the car!" he said, while waving the gun at me. I got out. "On your knees." he said. I kneeled. I felt the sand under me and inhaled the salty air of the beach. The wind was blowing, and it felt like everything was moving in slow motion. I thought to myself, my mother is going to pick up tomorrow's newspaper and read that a girl was found dead on the beach, and she's not going to know it's me.*

All I had was my tears. *"Stop crying!" he yelled.*

Stop crying? *"You've got to be out of your mind!" I thought. He pulled a gun on me because I didn't want to go out with a married man, and I couldn't cry about it. I am about to die. Finally, courage stepped in and I couldn't believe what I said next. "Just shoot me! Hurry up and get it over with." I felt that I was being tortured. The Lord was with me. "No weapon that is formed against thee shall prosper" (Isa. 54:17).*

All of a sudden, Sam told me to get back in the car. He drove back to my apartment and said, "Get out." I gladly jumped out of Sam's car. Psalm 56:8-11 says, "Thou tellest my wanderings put thou my tears into thy bottle: are they not in thy book? When I cry unto thee, then shall mine enemies turn back: this I know; for God is for me. In God will I praise his word: in the LORD will I praise his word. In God have I put my trust: I will not be afraid what man can do unto me".This experience was one of the most defining moments in my life. The Lord formed man out of the dust of the ground and breathed into his nose the breath of life and man became a living soul (Gen. 2:7). I read that gold was trapped in the Earth's core when the earth was formed. There is a little gold dust in us all, which is my humble opinion.

If you were to speak to a gold refiner today, they would tell you that at the end of the process the gold will look like mud; they would also tell you not to throw it away because that's real gold. Refining companies receive bars as well as scrap gold and liquefy the metal in a hot furnace. Workers then add borax and soda ash to the molten metal, which separates the pure gold from other metals. (www.gold-traders.co.uk/gold -information/how-to-refine-gold.asp). Think about this, the next time you go through the furnace, remember that God is removing some impurities from you. "Beloved, think it not strange concerning the fiery trial which is to try you, as though some strange thing happened unto you" (1 Peter 4:12).

During the California Gold Rush of 1845-1855, when gold was found by James W. Marshall at Sutter's Mill in Colona, California, the news of gold brought about 300,000 people from the rest of the United States and abroad (https://en.m.wikipedia.org/wiki/ California_Gold_Rush). I'm hoping that we can rush to see the value of our souls, because what good would it do to "gain the world and lose our soul?" (Matt. 16:26). What "would you give in exchange for your soul?" (Matt. 16:26) People left their families and traveled over dangerous territories at the prospect of gold. First Peter 2:29 states, "[ye] are a chosen generation, a royal priesthood, an holy nation, a peculiar people; that ye should show forth the praises of him who hath called you out of darkness into the marvelous light."

My husband once preached a sermon titled, *"What are You Looking For?"* *He explained how people are always looking for something- love, money, fame, anything except what really matters. I wish that others' would treat Jesus like people treated the Gold Rush of 1845. Come and stake your claim. "Now if any man build on this foundation gold, silver, precious stones, wood, hay, stubble, every man's work shall be made manifest. For the day shall declare it because it shall be revealed by fire and the fire shall try every man's work of what sort it is." (I Cor. 3:12-13)*

It takes a lot of courage to live a Christian life. A life of gold- pure refined gold, not fool's gold or pyrite (which glistens but doesn't shine). When you make bad decisions, whether through your speech or the way you dress, it takes courage. You have the power to choose your path and it is going to take courage. If you don't cast a vote for Jesus Christ, you are voting for fool's gold. Align your spirit with Jesus' because to him, *you are more precious than gold.*

Chapter 11

Wisdom

Pearl

Pearls come in a wide variety of colors. The most familiar of colors are white, cream, pale pink, and even a yellowish brown. Black, gray and silver pearls are also common, but overall the palette of colors can extend to just about every hue. In this particular chapter I am going to detour a little from the previous chapters, because wisdom is not limited to one's ethnicity or age. Wisdom is the quality of being wise. It has the power to judge rightly and follow the sounds and course of knowledge, which was discussed in chapter three.

Pearls are the only jewel that is a product of a living organism, gathering in response to irritations and moving from its place of growth to become an item of adornment ("...a horn like organic substance that is the main constituent of the mollusk's outer shell"), and secreting cells of the mollusk are located in the mantle or the epithelium of the body when the foreign particles penetrate the mantel and the cells attach to the particle and build up more concentric layers (a pearl) around it (https://micro.magnet.fsu.edu).

We (humankind) have similarities to the pearl. We should grow in the pearl of wisdom when "irritations of foreign particles" penetrate our lives. We may find ourselves facing a multitude of situations, including divorcing the love of our lives, serving as a caregiver with the world on our shoulders, helping a loved one facing an addiction, or grieving the death of a loved one. Whatever the situation, we are like the pearl. We are alive and one day we are going to move from Earth to glory to become a prized possession; for,

"[We] are bought with a price" and are not our own (1 Corinth. 7:32). When you become a Christian, you are accepting the Father, the Son, and the Holy Spirit as one. *We accept Jesus Christ as our savior, but I find that the problem with most people is that we have a problem with him being the Lord of our lives. Metaphorically speaking, you are the pearl. "Wisdom crieth without; she uttereth her voice in the streets..." (Proverbs 1:20). Are you listening? Get to know wisdom when you hear it- don't let wisdom go in one ear and out of the other.*

One afternoon, I decided to stop by the thrift store on my lunch break. As I stood at the jewelry counter looking at a pair of earrings, a woman walked up behind me. "Sometimes, you find pearls in these- they also offer good luck." She was speaking to the clerk, as she placed a small box on top of the jewelry counter. For some reason, the lady walked away from the box, and left it at the jewelry counter. I asked her if she was going to purchase the box and she replied, "No, I'm not going to buy it." I picked up the box. I didn't know what to expect to find inside, but I decided to purchase both the box and the earrings I had been looking at.

I walked to my car and decided that I wanted to open the box. The box was black in color, and when opened it I was surprised to see a small can and can opener inside it. When I opened the can, I saw that there was an oyster inside a pool of water. I pried the oval-shaped oyster open and jabbed at the lifeless grey meat but nothing happened. It felt wet and gooey, like play dough. I then squeezed the outer rim of the oyster and still nothing happened. The woman from the jewelry counter walked past my car and said, "Good Luck!" I smiled and continued to poke the inner parts of the same oyster until a small pink pearl popped out! This felt completely random. Minutes ago, I was pearl-less, and now I held a rare gem. Such is life- just like the rhythm of our heartbeat, life fluctuates. The natural rhythm of our lives is up and down. Remember, a complete stranger can point you in the direction of your pearl.

I excitedly ran into the store yelling, "I found a pearl! I found a pearl!" The clerk from behind the counter examined the beautiful pink pearl that was lying in my hand and before I knew it, my discovery started to draw attention.

Women were raising their voices saying, "I can't believe it's really real!" A man asked if he could have it.

Then, in the middle of the crowd, I threw my hands in the air, holding the pearl tightly and cried out, "THANK YOU LORD!" I ran back to my car and drove back to work. Before this discovery I was having a bad day at work, and now I had received this beautiful and most unexpected gift from God. I ran into work showing all of my co-worker's my beautiful pearl and then grabbed my phone to call my husband.

Just like I was excited to share the news of my pearl with everyone, I thought about how we should be just as excited to share the gospel with others'. In

Luke 24:13, Jesus was crucified on the cross and buried in a tomb; after the third day the stone was rolled away, and His body was gone; Afterwards the angels told three women that Christ had risen. These three women were Mary Magdalene, Joanna, and Mary (the mother of Jesus). When they were told that Jesus had risen, the news spread quickly. In verse thirteen, there were two disciples walking on the road to a small town called Emmaus when Jesus Christ himself joined them. They were talking about current events and had no idea at the time who they were speaking with. They were speaking with Christ, the one who gives wisdom liberally, for he said in James 5:5, "if any of you lack wisdom, let him ask God that giveth to all men liberally' and upbraideth not and it shall be given him."

God had prevented them from knowing who Christ was. They talked about the death, the burial, and the resurrection and how Christ would redeem Israel. They went on about how it was the third day of the resurrection; the three women were waiting by Jesus's tomb and how the angels told them that Christ was alive. Verse 25 then says, "...O fools, and slow of heart to believe all that the prophets have spoken..." (Luke 24:25). Jesus began teaching them the scriptures and went on to stay with them. "...he sat at the table with them, he took bread, he blessed it, and brake, and gave to them. And their eyes were opened, and they knew him..." (Luke 24:30).

Wisdom is crying out, but *why is she crying? I believe that our society, our world, our way of living, has made her sad. Is she weeping out of grief? Of course! I be-lieve she is shouting at us because very few people are listen-ing to her pleas. Wisdom calls, but don't forget that there are other ways to communicate: computer, radio, and television. Be advised that wisdom refuses to continue being ignored or hung up on, because one day you will no longer hear from her. "Again, the kingdom of heaven is like a merchant seek-ing beautiful pearls, who, when he has found one pearl of great price when he sold all he had and bought it" (Matt. 13:45-46). Revelations 21:21 says, "And the twelve gates were twelve pearls; every several gate was of one pearl: and the street of the city was pure gold, as it were transparent glass." Wisdom is telling you that you want to be inside of the beautiful gates of heaven; you want to hear God say, "… Well done, good and faithful servant…" (Matt. 25:21).*

One day my husband and daughter were exiting the highway, when a man ran towards the car waving his hands wildly. However, they couldn't hear him be-cause they were too far away. As the man got closer to the car, they could hear him shouting, "STOP!" My husband immediately hit the brakes. In front of the car was a baby, who had fallen out of a car. Soon after, a car pulled up and a woman jumped out, running fran-tically towards them. The baby had fallen out of her car and was still strapped in the car seat. The man who had waved them down, was a gentleman who was usually seen begging for money with a sign that read, *Money for Food. We do not know when a valuable pearl will be found, but thankfully, in this situation, my husband lis-tened to wisdom. Wisdom (pearl) was crying and shouting and begging in the streets (Pro. 1:20).*

Chapter 12

Joy

Jasper

Jasper, a microgranula quartz is a square mineral that is an opaque and impure variety of silica, usually red, yellow, brown, or green in color (and rarely blue) [www.geologylearn.blogspot.com/2016/12/jasper.html?m=1]. Joy, is a feeling of great pleasure and happiness (www.Google.com).

On Good Friday I went to the bank to check on my money, not because my money was working for me, but because I had to work my money (I was broke). I had to make sure I wasn't robbing Peter to pay Paul or bouncing checks. After taking care of this, I noticed a lady inside the bank selling jewelry. She was wearing a lot of jewelry and wore a salt and pepper haircut. Her makeup was flawless and she was wearing a black pant suit with suede ankle boots. Her frame was small and she was short in stature. There was jewelry everywhere; it was beautiful, high-end costume jewelry. I stopped only to admire it because I didn't have the money to purchase anything. I was content about that because my bills were paid. At that moment, an older woman with a big smile walked over to me and asked in a very southern tone, "Can I help you?"

I replied, "Oh, no ma'am, I'm just looking."

Our eyes met and she then said, "Oh, you are a child of God, you need some bling-bling! Pick out whatever set you want!"

In my mind, I thought it was one of those hidden camera jokes. I didn't move immediately, instead I said a little prayer to the Lord and explained to him that I wasn't ungrateful, but I would like a nice set of jewelry to go with some of my Sunday outfits. It was almost scary because I thought to myself, okay, I'm in the bank where there is a lot of money (little of which was mine) and this woman just told me to pick up something that wasn't mine and leave the bank with it? Just then, my son walked into the bank for which I am thankful because I needed a witness. Once I explained the situation to him, he asked me which pieces of jewelry did I like. I was in such a stupor, that I could not move. My son continued to help me pick out some jewelry pieces, while I was still in shock. I began to think about how God had heard my prayer and smiled on me that day. I cried, not because I was receiving the jewelry, but because the Lord had heard me. The woman hugged and consoled me, while my son burst out singing "God has smiled on me." The bystanders at the bank walked over and listened to his angelic voice singing praise unto the Lord. A short while later, we walked out of the bank with five bags of jewelry, all free. Before we left, the woman and I exchanged numbers. A few weeks later she called and told me she had another jewelry set for me to match my Easter Sunday outfit. Don't get me wrong, I did not keep all five bags of jewelry for myself, instead I shared that jewelry with some of my friends because I wanted to spread my blessings and joy with others.

A young lady and I used to work for the state and our job was to help others who were addicted to eating food. These patients were so overweight that we were instructed to make sure every cabinet and pantry was securely locked. We never realized how severe their eating disorder was until one day, I sat down to eat lunch and before I knew it, a lady sitting near me snatched my hot dog and swallowed it. I couldn't process what had happened quick enough. The purpose of the home was to try to integrate them back into society. The only problem, however, was that every job was associated with food in some way. One woman was given a job to watch over babies, and all of the formula bottles began to come up missing, and we later found out that she was drinking the formula out of the bottles. Another woman had eaten so much food that she ended up in a coma. Addictions are very powerful, not just food addictions, but other ones also. Most of the time, people are looking for something that gives them joy. It doesn't matter what kind of job you have, or how much money you have- addictions can affect any person from any background.

People usually base their joy on how they feel. It should be based on the things you know. On any given day, you could wake up and feel quite awful. The joy, however, comes knowing that God has blessed you with another chance of life. Another chance to breathe the breath of life. You have to know that God loves you and "will never leave or forsake [you]" (Heb. 13:5). You have to know that all things work for your good. You have to know when you are being tested and how you are going to get through the test. In Matthew 4, when Jesus was being tested in the wilderness, he was hungry. He had fasted for 40 days and for 40 nights. Satan approached Jesus and told him if he was the Son of God he could just turn the stones into bread. Jesus replied telling him that man should not live by bread alone but by the word of God. We should not base ourselves on how we are feeling, but instead follow the daily instruction of our heavenly father.

One of my former coworkers, Amy, was a drug and alcohol counselor. She counseled others about the 12 step program (www.recovery.org/topics/alcoholics-anonymous-12-step/), meant to help them with drug and alcohol addictions by:

1. Admitting they were powerless in controlling their alcoholism.
2. Admitting they needed a higher power to give them strength.
3. Recognizing their alcoholic past.
4. Making amends to all of those affected by their alcoholism.
5. Learning to live a new life with new behaviors.
6. Helping others who suffer with the same problem.
7. Making a moral inventory of ourselves.
8. Continue to make a moral inventory of self and admit when we are wrong.
9. Ask for knowledge and wisdom through your higher power source.
10. Continually praying and making a change in our lives.
11. After having our spiritual awakening and change, try to continue helping those who are also in need.
12. Humbly ask God to remove our shortcomings.

Amy would teach others about sobriety during the week, and she would give in to *her addiction and become drunk from Friday to Sunday. She would get really drunk and pass out. They would find her in the middle of the floor. She is what I call a functional alcoholic; she would wake up Monday and work a normal work week and when Friday evening came, she would succumb to her alcoholic tendencies again until Sunday night. I tried to talk to her about the steps, especially step 1 in which the individual must admit he or she has a problem. But Amy could not admit that she had a problem. As I got to know her better, I found out that her husband had been a heroin addict, and throughout the years she became disappointed in him and with her life, so she began to drink. She used alcohol to numb the feelings she generally kept to herself. "But I keep under my body, and bring it into subjection: lest that by any means, when I have preached to others, I myself should be a castaway" (1 Cor. 9:27).*

Speaking to others with addictions helped me realize they usually have some underlying, deep hurt that they are trying to cover up or mask. The addiction serves as their temporary joy. For instance, one of my alcoholic cousins joined a gang when he was younger. They broke into a home and he fired his gun to scare an unsuspecting visitor away, but the stray bullet hit and killed an infant. Like clockwork, he still gets drunk and talks about that night over and over again. He cannot forgive himself for what he did that night, and therefore he looks to alcohol as an opening to escape the pain he lives with every day. It's been about twenty years, but whenever we talk, I see that he cannot get rid of the past. For years, I have been trying to think of ways to convince him to forgive himself. We all have secret compartments where we dig and bury our shame and regrets in. Eventually, some of us are able to pack up that baggage and release it and say, "So what," Other people aren't able to do the same. When you cannot rid yourself from the past, you kill your future. When I look at my cousin, I realize that this situation has cost him relationships with his daughter, siblings, parents, and his career. He could have stepped out of the past, but instead, he was consumed by it. The shadows of death held him captive without release.

Addiction is a condition that causes a person to engage in a compulsive activity. It is my plea today that we addict ourselves to Christ. 1 Corinthians 16:15 says, "I beseech you brethren...that they have addicted themselves to the ministry of the saints." It is okay to let Jesus be your addiction. You will go through withdrawals from addictions to food, sex, alcohol, drugs, etc., but please choose to make Jesus your obsession, and he will serve as your permanent joy in life.

One day I saw a gentleman in the tag office who was suffering from PTSD. I can't remember how the conversation went, but he told me about all the places he had served and explained to me that he always likes to mess things up. As a little boy he would go hunting and he liked to shoot birds and squirrels. As a soldier, he liked the thrill of shooting guns, because it gave him an adrenaline rush.

He told me that he had orders to go on a mission to kill a group of men, and when they got to the place where the group was supposed to be, they followed the orders. Later they found out that they had killed a group of women and children instead. He told me that he felt really guilty about what happened, and has since been diagnosed with PTSD. There was one woman who managed to survive, and as they were trying to get her help, she made eye contact. Although he wasn't sure what ever happened to her, her face still haunts him along with the faces of the children.

War is not neat or polite. There was war in heaven because Satan wasn't content. I cannot believe he was able to swoon one-third of the angels to join his side! Well, they received their punishment and were forever kicked out of heaven (Rev. 12:9). Don't let Satan trick you out of your state of joy! Don't let him bamboozle you with feelings of depression or anxiety, because we can be with our heavenly father; "...the joy of the Lord is your strength" (Neh. 8:10).

Different colors have different frequencies and respond differently when applied to the body. Here is a list of how every color works on your body. The color may be applied to the body and can bring about a physiological and/or psychological change, ultimately restoring health.

*Yellow represents power and the body parts associated with yellow are the stomach, gallbladder, and liver.

*Blue represents the physical and spiritual aspects** of the mind and body as well as the means of communication throughout the body, and the parts associated with it are the ears, mouth, hands, and throat.

*Green represents love and responsibility,** and the body parts associated with it are the heart, lungs, and the thymus.

*Violet represents transmission, ideas, and information,** and the body parts associated with it are the pituitary gland, central nervous system, and the cerebral cortex.

*Red represents survival,** and the body parts associated with it are the gonads, kidneys and the sense of sight and smell. (www.empower-yourself-with-color-psychology.com/color-red.html)

Ironically, you are given a color based upon the month you are born. Those colors coincide with birthstones. The twelve birthstones that we know of today are actually derived from the 12 stones on Aaron's breastplate representing the twelve tribes of Israel. This is also said to be where we get our colors from. Revelations 21:19-20 says, "And the foundations of the wall of the city were garnished with all manner of precious stones. The first foundation was jasper; the second, sapphire; the third a chalcedony; the fourth, an emerald; The fifth, sardonyx; the sixth, sardius; the seventh, chrysolite; the eighth, beryl; the ninth, a topaz; the tenth, a chrysoprasus; the eleventh, a jacinth; the twelfth, an amethyst."

When we are seeking wisdom and light, we have to be careful because a lot of people want to use the meanings and origins of these stones in a way that God did not intend.

In Revelations 22:16 we are told that, "For without are dogs and sorcerers and whoremongers and murderers and, Idolaters and whosoever loveth and maketh a lie." If you are guilty of these when judgement comes, you will not get into heaven. 1 Samuel 28, Saul sought out a sorcerer to bring him out and in turn, became the Lord's enemy and lost his kingdom because he disobeyed God.

Conclusion

Bright Light Therapy

2 Peter 1:8 says, "For if these things be in you, and abound, that they make you that ye shall neither be barren nor unfruitful in the knowledge of our Lord Jesus Christ." If you are barren, you are unable to support growth (Imagine a lifeless and desert place!). Unfruitful means that you are unable to produce good or helpful results. Think of the many ways we use colors in our lives. We see them in every aspect of life: our national security team uses colors to dictate what level our nation's security is currently on; sororities and fraternities use colors to associate with the groups they are in; we use colors to support our favorite teams; and we also see the many colors used in the mysteries of nature. An elder of the church once said, "I don't understand how a spotted black and white cow can eat green grass and produce white milk, yellow butter, and end up having red meat." I also do not understand the how, when, where, and why of it all, but I understand the most important thing, and that is who God is. He is three in one: the father, the son, and the Holy Spirit.

In Luke 8:11-15, we read that the seed that must grow is the word of God. Satan is going to try and keep the seed from germinating, "…lest the world would believe and be saved (Luke 8:12) Some seeds will endure for a while and seem to have joy for some time, but with temptations they fall away because there are no roots planted firmly in the ground. The seeds have fallen on the hearts among thorns, which are choked by the cares, riches, and pleasures of life. Some seeds have fallen on the hearts of good ground. They have heard the word, adhered to it, and brought forth good fruit with patience. These are they that have fallen on good ground, converted with good and honest hearts: they take root and germinate, spreading the word of God among others. The word of God won't be barren or unfruitful if you have been adding these Christian graces with patience.

Naturally, when seeds are planted, they first grow roots. Once the roots take hold, a small plant will begin to emerge and eventually break through the soil. Without seeds, there would be no beautiful, colorful plants and fruit. Life would be barren. There are three things that a plant needs: light, food, and water. Light gives the small plants the energy it needs to begin photosynthesis. Photosynthesis is the process the plant uses to convert light energy into food. The seed lays dormant until water is added www.wonderopolis.com.

For spiritual growth, we also need the word of God. It will lay dormant when planted in our hearts until we hear (Rom. 10:17, Acts 15:7), believe (John 8:24, Heb. 11:5), repent (Acts 7:30-31), confess (Rom. 10:8-10) and add water- baptism (Acts 2:38, Rom. 6:1-5). We then add to our faith virtue, knowledge, temperance, patience, godliness, brotherly-kindness, and charity (2 Pet. 1:5). In order to become a tree of righteousness or a precious stone, we must let our light shine. The bible says not to put a candle under a bushel, but to let your light shine, in a brilliant hue "…before men that they may see your good works and glorify your father which is in heaven" (Matt. 5:16).

When wood becomes buried under volcanic ash, they lack oxygen and become petrified. "The mineral-laden water flowing through the covering material deposits minerals in the plant's cells; as the plants...decay. A stone mold forms in its place" (http://en.m.wikipedia.org/wiki/Petrified_wood).

The tree has transformed completely, from a living, breathing organism into a solid, petrified stone. We don't want to have a stony heart that stops our growth. A tree is known by the fruit that it bears. We know that if a banana turns brown, it is rotting and decreases in value. We also know that if the banana is green, it lacks nutrients and is not ready to be eaten. When a banana is yellow, it is ripe and at its full potential. The word of God must grow in our hearts. We must replace skepticism with faith, evil with virtue, misunderstanding and ignorance with knowledge; wildness with temperance; frustration and agitation with patience; sinfulness and blasphemous-ness with godliness; cruelty with brotherly kindness; and selfishness with charity.

When reading the bible, some people say that the red letters are more important because they were inspired by Jesus Christ. In reality however, "man should not live by bread alone but every word that proceedeth out of the mouth of God" (Matthew 4:4). The Old Testament was written for our learning, the New Testament is about how we are to live now, 2 Peter 1:21 states, that "...the prophecy came not in olden times by the will of man, but holy men of God spake as they were moved by the Holy Ghost." Let's be clear, the word of God does not give colors to these Christian graces. I am giving them colors, so if you are reading my book, you can connect and think about adding to your faith and becoming a tree of righteousness, because "The harvest is great, but the laborers are few" (Luke. 10:2).

We must address the lazy fruit pickers, which are people or situations in your life where Satan has used them to pick your fruit. Instead of producing their own fruit, they are going to try and shake you and take your beautiful, colorful fruit off your tree. Don't let Satan try to bring evil your way. He will try to agitate you, scandalize your name, stir up storms, tempt you, provoke you, discourage you and ultimately kill you. He will try to take the seed away before it has a chance to grow; like the bugs on a plant, Satan will try to eat your soul away. Sometimes, you may feel like you are planted beneath the dirt within the darkness. Just have patience- you will sprout roots and you will grow. We must be like a tree, planted by the rivers of the water: we shall not be moved *(Jer. 17:8)*. *Remember* that harvest time is coming. Always look towards the sun for growth. Revelations says that Christ will, *"thrust in [his] sharp sickle and reap; for the harvest of the earth is ripe..." (14:15)*. Christians, the farmers need to do their part to prepare for the harvest and bring the work of the Lord to completion; for we should be ready when the Lord descends to call us home and the faithful can bask in his light and worship him eternally in heaven.

Sherronda Bowman is an author, educator, playwright, personality coach, and motivational speaker. *Bright Light Therapy* is her first and proudest work. Native to Fort Lauderdale, Florida, she is a devoted wife, and loving mother and grandmother. She works by her beloved husband's side, who is a minister, evangelizing the word of God to others. The Lord has the first place in her heart and she is thankful to the Lord that she can share her journey with the world.

Poems

by Sherronda Boman

Because of the Sunlight

By Sherronda Bowman

Wearing a white gown around the throne of God is the entire or attire goal.

Even though, if you look closely, the gown is tattered and worn

But, I covered the rips with white lace.

I was only able to because I survived the side-walking crabs and the snakes that slid through the rocks with their charms and fangs of regret.

I shook them off and stepped over them once the manipulation multiplied them.

Spring will arrive and you will be able to bring some dying flowers and plants back to life because of the sunlight.

Are You Awake?

By Sherronda Bowman

Shall one wait until they wake to awaken to the weights of life?

Only when we provoke the love in others is the fullness of life enough to unite or suspend us.

How meaningful is your life?

How much will this world lose when death steals or kills us?

Have we waited on the tables of the issues of society, or the emotions that wars at a man's mind?

Can you serve your ball out of bounds and then adjust to the rules?

When we breathe, it should be God's praise.
As I lay at the wake, am I awaken to the true blessings?

Throw your ball, play life fairly.

Only then can we awaken to the Hallelujah of my purpose.

One truly never dies as long as memory lives and praises to God have been painted.

Or, has your life just waited for the wake?

All On Me

By Sherronda Bowman

Between the rolling in and out of the tides of life's ocean, we get glances of ourselves- the angles of our soul's mirror.

We catch places that we know exist, yet we've never seen before.

Sometimes, these reflections are picked up by mirrors positioned only by the slowing of our cadence or chipped pride.

Maybe even a false judgment or a dream that's a true nightmare.

Maybe not naked often, or taken time to examine ourselves, we realize, we often dress ourselves in the dark.

But how do I admit that our right, our light, and our time is wrong?

You must redress your life.

It's never too late, as long as you can admit it.

Because there's no If's, I Love You

By Sherronda Bowman

If I became skinny like a supermodel or changed my hair color to blonde, would you love me?

If I grew two inches taller and looked you in the eye- and my eyes were blue, would your song be true?

If I had the confidence with the air of arrogance, if I had money that could change your lifestyle, if I had power- would I alone have your heart and admiration?

And all the chambers of your imagination?
Could I steal your heart? Lust? Temptation?
Adoration?

Because I would love you if you were poorer than a pauper or poor in spirit.

I would love you if your body enlarged in size, through health issues, I would nurse and nurture you.

If you were blind, I would love you enough to be your eyes.

If you didn't have a voice, I would speak for you.

I would because: I Love You.

My Prayer

by Sherronda Bowman

The Lord is my brightness of the light when darkness camped out around my spirit.

Thy light never flickered.

The darker my midnight, your blinding light helps me see.

Oh Lord, give me your light so that I may give it to others.

Help me to dispel the darkness.

Light travels into the universe; help me to follow your path.

Let every attribute of darkness be uncomfortable.

Never blot out my candlestick.

This light isn't a transformed light alone.

Help me to follow the father of lights.

The Bright Light Therapist
by Royalle Bowman

Acknowledgements

from Sherronda Bowman

I want to acknowledge the Father, Son, and Holy Spirit because they acknowledge me everyday. I would like to thank my husband Bradley Bowman because he becomes a better man everyday and seems to be renewed day by day. He continues to work seven days a week showing his great love for me and his family. I am most proud of him preaching the gospel in season and out of season. I am truly proud to stand by him and be his wife.

I would like to thank my son Royalle' Bowman for his creativity and talent. I love the artwork. You truly have grown into a great man.

I would like to thank my daughter Helen Skye "Butterfly" Bowman for her business sense and for the courage to be a woman of honor.

I would like to thank my best friend Marilyn Dunlap for pushing me to write this book and holding my feet to the fire.

I would like to thank Brianna Dozier and LaToya Price for helping me to meet deadlines and being angels here on earth.

Armani Valentino, you treated me like an expecting mother. Thank you for pushing me when it was painful, and helping me to breathe through stressful deadlines.

Last but certainly not least I would like to thank my mother Bernice Mitchell for teaching me to walk by faith before I could actually walk. Also, for her wisdom and in depth knowledge of the scripture. I'm thankful for the conversations we have about the Word of God.

To order wholesale or bulk copies:
972-383-9234 or 972-781-8404

COLLEGE BOY
PUBLISHING

"We Breed Bestsellers"